Praise for Write Talk

GW00786491

Professor Joe O'Hara, Head of the School c
Dublin City University

'As someone who spends most of their professional life working with words, it is wonderful to have an easily accessible resource that facilitates the production of clear, concise and grammatically correct writing.

Write Talk is immediately relevant to the academic sphere but I would also argue that it is an essential companion for anyone who has been tasked with writing a report, making a presentation or even crafting a letter. You will find this book indispensable and I am delighted to be in a position to recommend Write Talk by DCU School of Education graduate, Fiona O'Murchú.'

Tony Donohoe, Head of Education and Social Policy IBEC

'A growing number of employers are voicing their concern about falling standards in written communication amongst their staff.

Accurate communication makes good business sense and reflects credibility and attention to detail, especially in emails and letters where the tone and culture of a business is set.

Write Talk is a valuable companion for everyone who wants to communicate with clarity, style and precision.'

Dr Denis Flannery, Senior Lecturer in English and American Literature, University of Leeds, England

'If the management of dress-code and formal letter-writing in the age of text-speak and the Internet are now and then beyond your grasp, then Fiona O'Murchú's new book is an enviably lucid guide.

'Write Talk' is a book not only for those who need guidance in relation to 'literacy' at its most generously defined. It is also invaluable for teachers, lecturers, coaches, mentors - anyone who aspires to help others towards mastery of these basic, and sometimes elusive, skills. This is a book I will be referring to in my own work and one I will be recommending to students and to colleagues.'

Gay White, Organisational Psychologist and Chairperson of the Dublin City University Alumni Council

'If you need to write, you need a copy of Write Talk on your bookshelf. It is a simple, clear and easily understood guide to all aspects of writing and communication. This book should be required reading for students at all levels. It would also be very useful for anyone who has to write as part of their job and simply needs to check a grammatical point. There are also some great tips for making presentations.
There is no doubt that I will have a copy of this permanently to hand when I find myself writing formally.'

Moira Cardiff, Development Education Officer of Poetry Ireland

'Write Talk is an essential reference guide for those of us who care about the English language. Students, graduates, teachers and those of us in between, lovers of words, budding writers, poets, crossword puzzlers and proof readers ... make sure to keep a copy in your bag!'

Micheál Duffy, Student, St. Oliver's Community College, Drogheda

'I like using Write Talk because you can rapidly access the contents page and from there you can quickly skip through to the section you are looking for. I use the book to help me figure out some confusing words that sound similar and to help me choose the right words that I need. When I was writing an essay for English, it was handy to quickly check some doubts I had about apostrophes. There's also some really handy information about formal letter writing.'

Mark Hanna, English and History Student, University College Dublin

'As a student, I've found Write Talk to be a very helpful tool in ensuring accurate spelling and grammar in essays and assignments. This book is an extremely useful guide to the common errors in written composition; but also demonstrates how people can fall into these mistakes.
Write Talk is a comprehensive, clear and concise textbook that I would recommend to my fellow students.'

www.writetalk.ie

Write Talk

Quick Reference Guide
to Writing and Communication

Fiona O'Murchú

Twiss Publishing

2nd Edition

ISBN: 978-1-5262-0146-1

Published by Twiss Publishing, Ireland 2016
www.writetalk.ie

Printed by Essentra, Glasnevin, Dublin 11

Contents

Writing Skills

Spelling

Oral, Aural and Visual Communications

Non-Verbal Skills

Digital Communications

Examination Vocabulary

British and American English Spelling Differences

Acknowledgements

Many thanks to Kevin Joyce (Principal), Sinead McDonnell (Deputy Principal) and my friends and colleagues in Bush Post Primary School, Co. Louth, for piloting this book and providing suggestions, opinions and encouragement.

Thanks also to Moira Cardiff (Poetry Ireland), and teachers Fiona Duggan, Maeve O'Malley and Loraine Lawlor for their professional views, useful proposals and invaluable feedback.

Finally, a special thanks to my family and the many teachers, parents and students who were the inspiration for this book.

Introduction

We all need to write and speak well in order to communicate effectively and in today's online world it is all too easy for a message to be misinterpreted.

Write Talk allows you to quickly check the main rules and conventions of British English and can be used for writing or speaking on any subject.

This book will help to set a professional tone to all your written and verbal communication. It will help you to write and speak with confidence and reflect accuracy, credibility, clear thinking and attention to detail. The clearly designed headings, subheadings and bullet point examples make it easy to navigate and its small size makes it practical for day-to-day use. The book is designed to dip in and out of when preparing work such as school or college assignments, projects, reports, letters, emails or presentations.

Write Talk contains the rules of punctuation, main parts of speech, grammar, spelling strategies and also guidelines on verbal and non-verbal communication. The conventions on writing formal letters and emails are listed and definitions of examination vocabulary are included.

Write Talk aims to support students and professionals develop good literacy habits and pave the way to exam success and professional achievement.

Rules for Capital Letters

In British English we use capital letters to indicate the importance of certain words. This can help us to become orientated with a text and allow us to understand it more easily. Nowadays, you often see the widespread misuse of capital letters, for example on the Internet, in business documents and in advertising.   However, the rules for using them have never changed.

Where to Use Capital Letters
Use a capital letter for:

- **I, when it refers to yourself**
  e.g. *I was at a meeting today.*
- **the first letter of a sentence**
  e.g. *The books were very expensive.*
- **days of the week and months of the year**
  e.g. *Monday, Tuesday, December, January*
- **principal words in titles of reports, books, plays, etc.**
  e.g. *To Kill a Mocking Bird, Romeo and Juliet*
- **the first letter of a direct quotation when the quote is a full sentence** e.g. *The boy asked 'Can I join your team today?'*
- **the word Internet as it is classed as a proper noun**
  e.g. *I was on the Internet for hours researching animals.*
- **the first letter of forenames and surnames** (proper nouns)
  e.g. *Sean, Michael Murphy, Lily Mae Edwards*
- **your own relatives when you use their title in place of their name** e.g. *'Have you seen Dad?' 'Where is Mum?'*
- **names of countries** e.g. *Ireland, Germany, China*
- **personal titles that come before a name** e.g. *Mr, Mrs, Dr*
- **titles of specific people**
  e.g. *President Michael D. Higgins, Captain James Cook*

- **names of companies or organisations**
  e.g. *Fyffes, Kingspan, Tesco*
- **main words in historical events**
  e.g. *The Battle of the Boyne, World War* II
- **names of religions** e.g. *Roman Catholic, Muslim, Buddhism*
- **places, towns, cities and buildings**
  e.g. *Clontarf, Killarney, Dublin, Empire State Building*
- **historical periods.**
  e.g. *Stone Age, Middle Ages, Ancient Egypt, The Renaissance*
- **monuments or landmarks**
  e.g. *The Four Courts, Blarney Castle, The Dublin Spire*
- **songs, films, poems, music**
  e.g. *Bohemian Rhapsody, The Titanic, Daffodils*
- **regions of a country** e.g. *Leinster, Yorkshire, Tuscany*
- **festivals and holidays**
  e.g. *Thanksgiving, Christmas, New Year's Day*
- **books and magazines** e.g. *The Hobbit, Reader's Digest*
- **languages** e.g. *Irish, French, Polish, Italian*
- **nationalities** e.g. *English, Spanish, French, South African*
- **the names of stars and planets** *e.g. Mars, Venus, Jupiter*
- **the initials BC and AD** indicating Before Christ and Anno Domini (Latin translated as: in the year of the Lord)
  e.g. *He lived around 850 BC.*
- **acronyms** e.g. *NATO, UNESCO, UNICEF*

Where not to Use Capital Letters

Do **not** use a capital letter for:

- **the names of school subjects or disciplines unless they happen to be the names of languages**
  e.g. *I prefer science and art to French and English.*

- **the title of a person when it is used in general terms and not connected to a specific person i.e. kings, queens, presidents**
  e.g. *A king always has the power to make final decisions.*
  I would love to become the president of our club.
- **the first letter of a quotation when it is a fragment or part of the sentence** e.g. *He said he was going to work to 'see the manager' to say goodbye.*
- **the second part of a direct quotation which is interrupted mid-sentence** e.g. *'Yes,' I said, 'it's a long way to travel.'*
- **most email addresses** *e.g. www.writetalk.ie*
- **the name of a general body rather than a specific one**
  e.g. *Each college has an academic council.*
- **the seasons** e.g. *Last summer we went to Galway.*
- **the compass points** e.g. *As we travelled north, the weather became colder.*

Unless they form part of a specific name
  e.g. *We travelled to the North Pole last year.*
  We visited South Africa two years ago.

Block Capitals

Block capitals are letters which are written separately in the shape of capital letters (see p.24). Block capitals are not normally used in everyday writing; however, we are often asked to fill in forms using them as they are easier to identify than cursive writing.

The general rule is not to:
- use block capitals unless you are instructed to do so
- use block capitals in emails as they may appear confrontational
e.g. PLEASE GET BACK TO ME AS SOON AS POSSIBLE

Punctuation

Punctuation marks are symbols that help us to read and understand text. They give meaning to words and phrases and inform us of the manner and tone in which a piece of text should be read.

A mistake with punctuation can give a piece of writing a totally different meaning e.g.:

- without punctuation: *'Lets eat Granny.'*
- with punctuation: *'Let's eat, Granny.'*

Note: The rules of punctuation never change!

Full Stop .

A full stop is normally used to break writing or text into sentences and to indicate a long pause while reading. This helps the reader to make sense of the text. A full stop is also known as a dot in computer terminology, a period in American English and a point in mathematics.

A full stop is used:

- **at the end of a complete sentence**
  e.g. *The car park was full today.*
- **after the initials in a name** e.g. *J. J. O'Neill   J. R. Tolkien*
- **after most abbreviations**
  e.g. *etc.   no.   a.m.   p.m.   i.e.*
- **outside brackets that contain a word or phrase**
  e.g. *We had a lovely day (despite the weather).*
- **inside brackets that contain a complete sentence**
  e.g. *Many of the children had a day off school (Class 3c were not off because they had an exam.)*
- **inside quotation marks**
  e.g. *'I love to spend my free time reading the newspapers.'*

- **when you abbreviate a word**
  e.g. *admin.* (administration) *bros.* (brothers)
- **after www in a web site address** e.g. *www.writetalk.ie*
- **to separate units from decimals** e.g. *12.4*
- **to separate euros from cents** e.g. *€27.89   €225.92*

You do <u>not</u> need a full stop:

- **if the sentence ends with a question mark or exclamation mark** e.g. *Where was the business meeting?*
  It looked like they were going to crash!
- **after headings or sub-headings**
  e.g. *Introduction   Chapter 2   Part Seven*
- **for titles** e.g. *title of a book: Write Talk*
                      title of a film: The Sound of Music
                      title of a poem: Daffodils
- **for abbreviated measurements**
  e.g. *kg   cm   mm   km*
- **after the abbreviations BC and AD** indicating Before Christ and Anno Domini (in the year of the Lord) e.g. *In the 1st century AD Europe was dominated by the Roman Empire.*
- **after capital letters used for abbreviations of companies, organisations and countries** (known as acronyms)
  e.g. *LMETB   ESB   GAA   NATO   USA*

Note: In British English we do not use a full stop after titles such as Mr, Dr, or Mrs but American English punctuation does.

Comma   ,

A comma is used to indicate a short pause while reading. It divides a sentence into parts making it easier to read and understand.

A comma is used:

- **to separate parts of a sentence and show the reader where to pause** e.g. *The road was flooded, but we got home safely.*
- **to separate items on a list (but not after the second last item)** e.g. *Remember to buy books, pencils, paper and pens.*
- **after introductory words or phrases** e.g. *Please, could you get my coat? Once upon a time, a princess lived in the castle.*
- **to separate things you do or places you go** e.g. *I arrived at work, ate my lunch, wrote some reports, went home and climbed into bed.*
- **before conjunctions such as: but, like, because, since, yet,** e.g. *He baked cakes, because he liked cooking.*
- **before direct speech** e.g. *The man said, 'Get out of here.'*
- **In place of a word which has been intentionally omitted** e.g. *The office was closed, both gates were locked.*
- **in large numbers after every third digit from the right** e.g. *25,000,000   €3,550,000   £1,000,000,000*

Semi Colon   ;

A semi colon is used to link related parts of a sentence.

A semi colon is used:

- **to join two short sentences without using a conjunction (link word) such as so, and, but.** e.g. *There was a presentation today; it took almost three hours.*
- **to connect closely related ideas** e.g. *Some people run wearing trainers; others run in their bare feet.*

Note: A semi colon is normally followed by a lower case letter.

Colon :

A colon is used to show an explanation or further details of something.

A colon can be used:

- **between two clauses when the second clause follows or explains the first**
  e.g. *It was difficult: in the end, I asked my brother to fix it.*

- **to prove a point**
  e.g. *Most schools offer a good education: you can check the results.*

- **at the end of an independent clause which is followed by a list** e.g. *He won all the top prizes: a car, a holiday and a camera.*

- **before a quotation and sometimes before direct speech**
  e.g. *The title of the book was: 'Safe Driving'.*
  The small child whispered: 'I want to go home!'

- **to introduce bullet points**
  e.g. *The following are key points from the meeting:*
  - *organise opening times*
  - *agree on ground rules*

- **to introduce a list**
  e.g. *Rory's Materials:*

  > *2 sheets plywood*
  > *1 box five mm screws*

- **to describe something** e.g. *It was a beautiful day: blue skies and a light breeze.*

- **to indicate a subtitle or a subdivision of a topic**
  e.g. *Cooking for Men: Joe's Experience*

Exclamation Mark !

An exclamation mark is used to indicate surprise, shock or strong feeling. You should use a capital letter after an exclamation mark the same way as you would after a full stop.

An exclamation mark is used:

- **to show anger** e.g. *'How dare you!'*
- **to show astonishment or surprise** e.g. *'I can't believe it!'*
- **to indicate a demand**
  e.g. *The small girl stamped her feet and screamed, 'I want that blue toy!'*
- **to indicate a command** e.g. *'Get out of my way!'*
- **to indicate sarcasm or humour** e.g. *... and then he said that the donkey sat down!*
- **to plea or appeal for something** e.g. *'Please can I go to the night club!' she begged her father.*

Note: Only one exclamation mark should be used in formal writing. You sometimes see two or more exclamation marks used but this should only be done in comic strips or personal writing.

Apostrophe '

An apostrophe is mainly used in two contexts: to show possession or ownership of something or to indicate the place where a letter or letters have been left out of a word (contraction).

For possession an apostrophe is used:

- **to show that something belongs to someone or something**
  e.g. *Ciara's books were on the floor.*
- **to show singular possession by placing it in between the last letter of a word and the s**
  e.g. *The golfer's shoes were in the corner. (one golfer)*

- to show plural possession (belongs to more than one person or thing) by placing the apostrophe after the s. e.g. *The golfers' shoes were in the corner. (more than one golfer)*
- before the s for plural words that don't end with s
  i.e. men, women, children, people
  e.g. *the men's coats*
  the women's handbags
  the children's shoes
  the people's decision

An apostrophe is also used:

- to indicate where a letter has been left out of a contraction (see p. 47).
  e.g. *The small child can't (cannot) reach the light switch.*
- for the contraction it's, meaning 'it is'
  e.g. *Shane discovered that it's (it is) a long way to Cork.*
- for abbreviated dates to indicate where numbers are missing
  e.g. *She got married back in '69.*
- between the 'o' and clock when writing the time of day
  e.g. *eleven-o'clock*
- to show the plural of single letters
  e.g. *How many m's are in management?*

Do not use an apostrophe:

- when forming plural words
  e.g. *The dogs and cats lived in the large kennels.*
  The CDs were kept in a box.
  Fathers and daughters have a special bond.
- for possessive pronouns
  e.g. *his, hers, yours, ours, theirs, its*

- **in decade years that are not abbreviated**

  e.g. *1700s   1850s   1920s   1970s*
- **in decade ages between the number and the letter 's'**

  e.g. *He was in his 20s when he graduated.*
- **for plural nouns**

  e.g. *rights and wrongs, boys and girls, tables and chairs.*

Note: Be careful not to confuse the contraction it's (it is) with the possessive pronoun its.

e.g. *It's going to rain today.   The dog is missing from its kennel.*

Quotation Marks   ' '

Quotation marks are used at the beginning and end of direct speech. They can also be used to highlight an unusual word or phrase.

Quotation marks are used:

- **for marking out direct speech by enclosing the actual words that are spoken**

  e.g. *Becky declared, 'I would love to visit Ireland.'*
- **after the final punctuation mark in direct speech**

  e.g. *Karen eventually asked, 'Who called to the office?'*
  His very words were 'I can't believe it!'
- **as double quotation marks when a second quote is used within direct speech** e.g. *His mother whispered 'Sean said "get out" during the argument.'*
- **to highlight a phrase or expression**

  e.g. *He decided to 'bite the bullet' and own up to his mistake.*

Do <u>not</u> use quotation marks for:

- **indirect quotations (reporting what someone said but not using their exact words)** e.g. *Susannah told me that it was very sunny when she went to school.*

Question Mark   ?

A question mark is used at the end of a question.

A question mark is used:

- **after a direct question**

  e.g. *'Where did you hide the present? '*

- **in place of a full stop when a direct question is asked**

  e.g. *'What were you going to say?'*

- **to turn a statement into a question**

  e.g. *She's going to the shop now?*

- **statements ending with a query**

  e.g. *'You will sweep the floor, won't you?'*

- **to indicate doubt about something** e.g. *He lived in Paris from 1929 (?) until his death in 1940.*

Do <u>not</u> use a question mark after:

- **an indirect question or reported question or query**

  e.g. *He wanted to know why I was going home.*

Ellipsis ...

An ellipsis is a series of three evenly spaced dots.

An ellipsis is normally used to indicate:

- **where one or more words have been intentionally omitted**

  e.g. *She opened the window ... perhaps he saw her.*

- **the omission of some words from a quotation or paraphrase**

  e.g. *According to Maslow, it is tempting ... to treat everything as if it were a nail.*

- **hesitation, lead in or trailing off of a thought or sentence**

  e.g. *I just meant ...*

Note: When an ellipsis is used after a full stop there are a total of four dots e.g. *The dog was big.... He looked at the photograph again.*

Dash —

A dash is a short horizontal line that can be used on its own or as a pair instead of brackets. It is used to indicate a mark of separation which is stronger than a comma. Dashes are more commonly used in informal writing such as notes, blogs or emails, but it is better to use them sparingly when you are writing formally.

A dash is used:

- **in dialogue to indicate a break in thought or tone**
  e.g. *'I thought you were going to' – Suddenly a large dog appeared. 'Where did he come from?' Ciara asked.*

- **in pairs, to show information or thoughts that are not essential to the rest of the sentence**
  e.g. *Lots of dogs – like those in the kennels – have been abandoned at Christmas.*

- **to indicate an additional piece of information**
  e.g. *She ate a big meal – steak, chips, peas, apple pie – and then went for a long walk.*

- **at the beginning of a sentence to indicate that you are continuing where you left off**
  e.g. *' – as I was saying, it is important to drive on the left side of the road.'*

- **at the end of a sentence to show where words have been omitted**
  e.g. *They were going to give him the job, but –*

- **to indicate a range of numbers.**
  e.g. *pages 29 – 255*

- **for a date when the time frame has not ended**
  e.g. *Mary M. 1959 –*

Hyphen -

A hyphen is smaller than a dash. There are no strict rules for using them however; there are guidelines that you can follow. The general rule is not to use a hyphen unless it is needed to clarify a word and help the reader to understand and pronounce it. There is no space on either side of a hyphen unless it is a hanging hyphen (see below).

A hyphen is used:

- **when a word is broken at the end of a line of text and continued on the next line (hanging hyphen)**
  e.g. *When the doctor arrived he took Peter's temper-*
  ature to see if it was too high.
- **to make compound words by linking words which have combined meaning**
  e.g. *mother-in-law, face-to-face, well-being, power-driven*
- **to join prefixes to words when they have adjoining vowels**
  e.g. *anti-aircraft, de-ice, re-enter, semi-automatic*
- **with a prefix before a proper noun or a date**
  e.g. *anti-British, post-World War I, pro-European, pre-1950s*
- **when words need clarification**
  e.g. *re-creation (creating again) as distinct from recreation (enjoyable pastime). Co-worker instead of coworker.*
- **when writing compound numbers ranging from twenty-one to ninety-nine** e.g. *Sixty-two people went on the train and twenty-five returned on the bus.*
- **when writing fractions in words**
  e.g. *It looked like three-quarters of the pizza had been eaten.*

Note: When breaking a word at the end of a line of text and inserting a hanging hyphen, the word should be broken between syllables and the hyphen placed at the end of the first part of the word.

Main Parts of Speech

Learning the different parts of speech can help us to understand sentence construction and assist us in recognising and correcting our own grammatical errors. This can help to provide a strong foundation for writing good English.

Speech can be divided into eight main parts:

1. **verbs**
2. **nouns**
3. **adjectives**
4. **adverbs**
5. **pronouns**
6. **prepositions**
7. **conjunctions**
8. **interjections**

Main Parts of Speech Explained

<u>**Verbs**</u> **are words that describe an action or a state of being.**
>   e.g. *Michael kindly **<u>fixed</u>** the red car.*
>   *Anne **<u>was</u>** good.*

<u>**Nouns**</u> **are the name of a person, place or thing.**
>   e.g. **<u>*Michael*</u>** *kindly fixed the red **<u>car</u>**.*

Three types of nouns are:

>   **proper noun:** the name of a particular person, place or thing.
>   **common noun:** general things e.g. *bread, table, dog, kettle etc.*
>   **abstract nouns**: describe ideas, qualities and conditions
>   e.g. *happiness, love, success, faith, progress etc.*

Adjectives describe a noun.

    e.g. *Michael kindly fixed the **red** car.*

Adverbs are words that modify a verb, adverb or adjective by providing more information about them. An adverb can be used to:
    modify a verb:
    e.g. *Michael **kindly** fixed the red car.*
    modify an adjective:
    e.g. *Michael kindly fixed the **big** red car.*
    modify another adverb:
    e.g. *Michael **very** kindly fixed the red car.*

Pronouns are used in place of nouns. Common pronouns are I, you, he, she, him, her, it, we, us, them and they.

    e.g. ***He** quickly fixed the red car.*

Prepositions are words which are used to indicate time and place.

    e.g. *Sarah left her lunch **in** the fridge.*
    *Peter put his shoes **under** the table **at** bedtime.*

Conjunctions (see p. 48) are words which are used to join parts of a sentence or phrase. Common conjunctions are:
but, so, although, and, because, when, just, for, until, since.

    e.g. *The office will open **when** the bus arrives.*
    *Robert kept his shoes on **until** bedtime.*

Interjections are used to show sudden emotion. Common interjections are Wow! Surprise! Gosh! Ouch!
They are often followed by an exclamation mark.

    e.g. ***Wow!** That was a great goal.*
    *When the lights went on we all shouted, **'Surprise!'***

Writing Skills

Handwriting

The emphasis on good handwriting has become less popular due to the advent of modern technology such as computers, printing and texting. Individual handwriting reflects personality; however, it is useless unless it is clearly legible.

The purpose of handwriting is to convey a message so it needs to be clear and legible in order to be understood. The correct shape should be used for each letter. Remember to be conscious of how you are writing, as a careful approach can embed good habits which will in time become automatic.

Upper Case Letters (Capitals or Block Capitals):

A B C D E F G H I J K L M N O P Q R S T U V W X Y Z

Lower Case Letters:

a b c d e f g h i j k l m n o p q r s t u v w x y z

Vowels:

a e i o u

Consonants:

b c d f g h j k l m n p q r s t v w x y z

The letter Y can be used as either a vowel or a consonant

Note: An easy way to remember where to use capital and lower case letters is to always use lower case lettering unless a capital is specifically required (see p.9-11).

Sentence Construction

A sentence is a group of words that are put together and make complete sense on their own. A sentence should express a complete thought.

A sentence must:

- contain a verb (action word)
- contain a noun (naming word - person, animal, place, thing or abstract idea)
- start with a capital letter
- end with a full stop, question mark or exclamation mark
- contain a subject i.e. who or what is doing the action being performed

A compound sentence:

- is made up of two simple sentences joined together by a conjunction (see p. 48). e.g. *The students were late for college and the lecturer was upset.*

Note: Compound sentences should not contain too many conjunctions e.g. *also, but, until etc.* as this will make them long and difficult to follow. You should avoid overuse of the word 'and'.

Paragraphs Explained

Paragraphs are used to group sentences together into separate sections, making the text easy to read and understand. They help the writer to organise thoughts in a clear and structured manner.

A simple way to remember where to use a paragraph is:

- one paragraph = one idea
- new paragraph = new idea

A paragraph:
- is a group of sentences which develop one point
- begins with a topic sentence which introduces a general idea
- starts when you change to a new time
- starts when you change to a new place
- starts when the speaker changes
- starts when you introduce a new topic
- should have sentences which develop a topic in a self-contained manner
- should vary in length
- leads the reader systematically from one point to the next
- can be used for dramatic effect to emphasise an important point
- should be indicated by leaving a blank line in between each new paragraph or by indenting the first sentence in a paragraph

Note: The first sentence of a paragraph should introduce the subject or topic. The rest of the paragraph should further explain that topic or subject.

Plural Nouns

There are a number of ways to make plural nouns.

Rules for making plural nouns:
- The most common way to make a plural noun is to add 's' or 'es' to the end of a word. e.g. *bag changes to bags and branch changes to branches.*
- If the noun ends with a vowel and a 'y' add 's' e.g. *boys.*
- If the word ends in 'ch', 'sh', 's', 'x', or 'z' the plural is usually made by adding 'es' e.g. *catch changes to catches.*

An **irregular noun** is a noun that becomes plural by changing its spelling in ways other than by adding 's' or 'es' at the end.

- If the noun ends with a consonant and a 'y', change 'y' to 'ies' e.g. *family changes to families.*
- If the word ends in an 'f' or 'fe' change them to 'ves'. e.g. *shelf changes to shelves, wife changes to wives*
- If the word ends in an 'o' such as potato or piano, there is no definite rule. It is better to learn these words individually. e.g. *potato becomes potatoes but piano becomes pianos.*

Some irregular plurals:

Singular	Plural
appendix	appendices
bacterium	bacteria
beau	beaux
bureau	bureaux
calf	calves
cactus	cacti
child	children
crisis	crises
criterion	criteria
curriculum	curricula
diagnosis	diagnoses
ellipsis	ellipses
foot	feet
formula	formulae
goose	geese
half	halves
index	indices
louse	lice
man	men
memorandum	memoranda
mouse	mice
nucleus	nuclei

oasis	oases
ox	oxen
penny	pence
person	people
phenomenon	phenomena
radius	radii
serum	sera
sky	skies
stimulus	stimuli
syllabus	syllabi
thesis	theses
tooth	teeth
woman	women

Some nouns have the same single and plural form e.g.:

aircraft	pike
barracks	salmon
buffalo	scissors
carp	series
deer	shambles
fish	sheep
haddock	shrimp
means	species
moose	swine
offspring	trout

Some nouns are only used in the plural form e.g.:

belongings	jeans	pyjamas
clothes	outskirts	scissors
congratulations	people	sunglasses
goggles	police	tights
headphones	premises	tweezers

Root Words

A root word is a basic word without any extra parts added on to the beginning or the end e.g. care is a root word. Learning to identify the root of a word may help us to learn spellings more easily. When a group of words share the same root they become a word family:

e.g. *care, caring, careful, careless, carefully, carer, carefulness, carefree, caress, uncaring.*

Note: You can make new words by adding different beginnings and endings to root words.

Prefix

A prefix is a word part which is placed at the start of a word. A prefix can change the meaning of a word.

- e.g. happy + prefix 'un' = unhappy
- e.g. advantage + prefix 'dis' = disadvantage

Common Prefixes

Prefix	Meaning	
anti	against	e.g. *antifreeze*
co	with or jointly	e.g. *co-driver co-operative*
de	remove	e.g. *defrost deflate*
dis	the opposite	e.g. *discontinue*
fore	before	e.g. *forecast*
inter	between	e.g. *interact*
micro	small	e.g. *microwave*
mid	in the middle	e.g. *midway midterm*
mis	wrong or bad	e.g. *misspelling misinterpret*
non	not	e.g. *nonsense*
post	after	e.g. *postoperative*
pre	before	e.g. *preschool*
pro	in favour of	e.g. *proactive*

re	again	e.g. *relive*
sub	lower position	e.g. *subsoil*
super	above/better	e.g. superhero
trans	across	e.g. *transatlantic*
ultra	extreme	e.g. *ultraviolet*
un	not	e.g. *untidy*

Suffix

A suffix is a word part which is placed at the end of a word. A suffix can change the meaning of a word.

- e.g. eat + suffix 'ing' = eating
- e.g. comfort + suffix 'able' = comfortable

Common Suffixes

Suffix	Meaning	
able / ible	is possible / can be done	e.g. *attainable*
ance	action, state or quality	e.g. *assistance*
ed	past tense verbs	e.g. *walked*
ent	someone or something that	e.g. *resident*
ery	type, group or place of work	e.g. *bakery nursery*
ful	full of	e.g. *hopeful*
ic	having characteristics of	e.g. symbolic
ics	body of facts or principles	e.g. *electronics*
less	without	e.g. *fearless*
ing	forms the present participle of verbs or adjectives e.g. singing, running, amazing, going, being etc.	
ment	action or process	e.g. *concealment*
ness	in the state of	e.g. *happiness*
ous	full of or having that quality	e.g. *boisterous*
ship	condition, skill or position	e.g. *leadership*

Alternative Words (Synonyms)

Many of us tend to repeat words such as 'said' and 'went' in our writing. The use of alternative words or phrases can help to extend vocabulary and expand our ideas.

The lists below offer some alternatives to commonly repeated words:

Some alternative words for said:

added	declared	muttered	revealed
admitted	demanded	pleaded	roared
advised	described	pondered	screamed
answered	discussed	protested	shouted
approved	exclaimed	ranted	shrieked
argued	explained	recited	snapped
asked	exploded	remarked	sobbed
boasted	hinted	replied	spluttered
chatted	hissed	reported	stuttered
commented	informed	requested	uttered
confessed	mentioned	responded	whispered
cried	mumbled	retorted	yelled

Some alternative words for went:

ambled	hurried	rushed	strolled
climbed	meandered	sauntered	trekked
dawdled	moseyed	staggered	waded
departed	rambled	stomped	wandered

Some alternative words for thought:

assumed	considered	deliberated	reflected
believed	contemplated	imagined	sensed

Some alternative words for saw:

examined	glared	peeped	spotted
eyed	looked	peered	stared
gazed	noticed	regarded	viewed
glanced	observed	scrutinised	watched

Some alternative words for good:

enjoyable	ideal	perfect	satisfactory
excellent	lovely	pleasant	superb
fine	nice	pleasing	wonderful

Some alternative words for bad:

appalling	disagreeable	foul	terrible
atrocious	dreadful	nasty	unpleasant
awful	evil	rotten	wicked

Some alternative words for nice:

agreeable	charming	fine	pleasant
amiable	cordial	good	pleasing
attractive	courteous	kindly	pretty
beautiful	enjoyable	lovely	warm

Some alternative words for quickly:

briskly	hurriedly	promptly	speedily
forthwith	immediately	punctually	straightaway
hastily	instantly	rapidly	swiftly

Some alternative words for big:

colossal	huge	immense	substantial
enormous	large	massive	vast

Writing Formats

There are many different ways of organising and presenting written communication. You should research and prepare your writing by drafting, reviewing, proofreading and revising your work until you are satisfied with it. Some writing formats are explained below:

Article: An article is a piece of writing which is usually published in some format such as a newspaper or magazine. It is intended for a wide audience. It normally contains a title, an interesting summary to grab the attention of the audience and the actual piece of work itself. Start an article by deciding on its purpose and identifying the audience or readership for whom it is intended.

Autobiography: An autobiography is the story of a person's life which is written by the person themselves.

Biography: A biography is the story of a person's life which is written by someone else.

Diary/Journal: A diary or journal is a record of events or experiences arranged by date. It can be used to record and track appointments and entries are typically short. A personal diary could contain personal thoughts, feelings and comments. An academic diary is a diary which starts at the beginning of the academic year – usually in August.

Drama: Drama is a composition in prose or verse which is written in a style suitable for performance.

Essay: An essay is a short literary composition in prose which is structured and generally focusses on a particular subject. Different styles of essay include:

- descriptive essay which creates a vivid picture of ideas, places or people. It describes thoughts, voices, sounds, feelings, characterisation, plot etc.
- expository essay which is factual and to the point and gives information e.g. *instructions or directions*. It should not contain descriptive detail or opinion.
- narrative essay which tells a story and is often used in a personal essay.
- persuasive essay which illustrates opinions and thinking skills and attempts to convince the reader to see things the author's way.

Fiction: Fiction is an imaginary piece of writing which deals with information or events that are not real. Two main types of fiction are realistic fiction and non-realistic fiction. Realistic fiction is written in a way that makes the story seem believable in real life even though it is untrue e.g. *Historical Fiction*. With non-realistic fiction it is obvious that the story or events could not happen in real life e.g. *Science Fiction, Fantasy, Fairy Tales.*

Memoir: A memoir is a collection of memories or events personally experienced by the author. It is a piece of non-fiction written in the first person from the author's point of view. A memoir differs from an autobiography in that it does not tell the story of an entire life but focusses on a particular aspect or event in a life.

Minutes: Minutes are the written records which are taken during a meeting or hearing. They should summarise the main points rather than giving a word for word account of events. Minutes should include the date, a list of all those present, the issues discussed, the responses and any decisions taken. Minutes provide a permanent record for future reference.

Non-fiction: Non-fiction is a piece of writing based on real life events. The author believes the facts to be true at the time of writing.

Poetry: Poetry is a form of writing that expresses the beauty of language. It often uses symbolism, image and rhythm to evoke meaning.

Proposal (written): A proposal is a written request. It is a way of putting forward an idea or asking for permission to do something. A proposal should state the purpose of the request or idea, give some background information and also contain specific information about the suggestion.

Report: A report is a systematic well organised document which analyses a topic or problem. It should contain accurate information such as facts and findings and be concise, clear and well structured. Personal opinions should not be included unless they have been specifically requested.

Review: A review is a description and evaluation of a book, film, play, game etc. It should be a commentary rather than a summary. You can identify parts that you agree or disagree with and comment on what you like or dislike. It is important to clearly state your own opinions and support them by giving examples. A general layout contains: introduction, description, opinions and recommendations.

Summary (synopsis): A summary is a concise explanation of a larger piece of work such as a book, speech or story. It should contain a brief account of all the main points and not go into them in any great detail. When writing a summary you must be careful not to change the meaning of the information which you are summarising.

Formal Letters

A business letter should be written in a formal style of writing and be presented in a professional, polite and courteous manner. Clichés such as 'at the end of the day' and 'at this point in time' etc. should be avoided when writing formal letters.

You should always plan your letter by making rough notes, writing a draft, reviewing and proofreading it and making any necessary changes before writing or typing the final letter.

The main conventions of formal letter writing are:

- Write your own address in the top right hand corner.
- Write the date under your own address.
- Always write the date in the long format. e.g. *25th July 2015*
- It is always advisable to find out the name of the person you wish to write to and use their name in the greeting.
- The address of the person to whom you are writing should be placed on the left below your own address.
- When adding a reference line to a business letter it should be placed on the left between the recipients address and the salutation. Leave one space above and below this line.
- Possible ways to start a letter are:
    - 'Dear Sir', or 'Dear Madam', if you know you are writing to a man or a woman but don't know the name of the person.
    - Dear Sir / Madam – if you don't know who you are writing to.
    - To Whom It May Concern - This is usually used in a letter which is likely to be given to anyone and it doesn't matter who reads it.
    - Dear Mr (surname), Dear Mrs (surname) – use this when you know the name of the person.

- o Use Ms for a woman unless you are specifically asked to use or know the person as Miss or Mrs.
  - o Dear Kevin – use a forename for a close business colleague or friend.
- Spell names correctly and always use the person's title.
  e.g. *Dear Dr Smyth, Dear Ms Byrne*
- If you have enclosed anything in the letter you should refer to it e.g. *I have enclosed ... (enc. or encl.)*
- When typing a letter, sign your name at the end and then type your name underneath. This will ensure that the reader has the correct spelling of your name.
  e.g. *Mary Smyth*
  Mary Smyth
- Possible ways to conclude a formal letter are:
  - o I look forward to hearing from you.
  - o Please do not hesitate to contact me.
  - o If you require any further information...
  - o Enclosed you will find...
  - o Please feel free to contact me at (email address or telephone number).
  - o You can contact me at the above address.
  - o I look forward to hearing from you in the near future.
- Ways to sign off:
  - o Use 'Yours faithfully' if you do not know the name of the person you are writing to:
    e.g. *Dear Sir / Madam - Yours faithfully*
  - o Use 'Yours sincerely' if you know the name of the person you are writing to:
    e.g. *Dear Mr Dunne - Yours sincerely*

Note: If you need to use a less formal method of signing a letter off, you can use Regards, Kind regards or Best wishes etc.

Layout of a Formal Letter:

> **Your**
> **address**
>
> **Date** in long format
> e.g. 3rd August 2015
>
> **Address of person** you are writing to
>
> If you have a reference, membership or policy number put it here
> e.g. Re: Policy No. 123456
>
> **Dear Sir / Madam** or name of person
>
> **First paragraph** - Introduce yourself and say why you are writing.
>
> **Next paragraph/s** - more detail about the purpose of your letter.
>
> **Final paragraph** - conclude and give your contact details in this
> paragraph if appropriate to the letter.
>
> **Sign off** with 'Yours faithfully' if you **<u>do not</u>** know the name of the
> person you are writing to e.g. Dear Sir: Yours faithfully
>
> **Sign off** with 'Yours sincerely' if you have used the person's name
> e.g. Dear Mr Thompson: Yours sincerely
>
> **Sign your name** at the end of the letter.
> When typing a letter, type your name under your signature in order
> to ensure that the reader can read and spell your name correctly.

Always proofread your letter before sending it. Remember that it is
easier to proofread from a hard copy.

Common Abbreviations in Writing

An abbreviation is a shortened form of a word/s or phrase. In general, when an abbreviation consists of the first letter of a word, or the first and last letters of a word e.g. UK, ATM, Mr, Ltd, it does not require a full stop. However, if the abbreviation consists of the first section of a word you should use a full stop e.g. Fri. Jan. prof.

Some common abbreviations used in writing:

- **attn** is used to draw your attention to something or someone's name. It is often used in business correspondence such as letters.
- **cc** means carbon copy. It is used to indicate that one or more copies have been produced and sent to people other than the main recipient. In an email it indicates that a copy of the message has been sent to the person/s named in the cc box.
- **c/o** means care of. It is used at the beginning of an address on a letter or parcel if you are sending it to someone at another person's address. e.g. *Mr Smyth, c/o Handy Hair, 8 Park Street, Dublin.*
- **e.g.** means 'for example'. Use it to indicate an example. e.g. *Various types of books are available in the shop* e.g. *autobiographies, biographies, fiction and non-fiction.*
- **enc**. means that something is enclosed. It is generally used in a note or letter to indicate that something extra is enclosed.
- **etc**. means and so on. e.g. *There were lots of animals at the show: dogs, horses, sheep etc.*
- **FAO** means for the attention of.
- **i.e.** means 'that is'. It is used to explain something e.g. *I am going to keep my work in a safe place, i.e. the staff room.*
- **NB** means take note of or pay attention to e.g. *NB: The room won't be open until 2pm.*

- **PS** means postscript or written after. It is often used at the end of a letter or message to indicate that more information or an afterthought has been added in.
- **pp** indicates that a document or letter has been signed on behalf of another person. For example, a deputy may sign documentation when the manager is unavailable and they can use pp to indicate that this has been done.
- **PTO** means please turn over. It is generally used at the end of a page to indicate that more information is on the reverse.
- **re** means regarding or in the matter of. It is typically used in the heading of business letters or emails to indicate the main topic of the message. It is usually placed at the top of the message. A colon is generally used after re (e.g. *re:*).
- **via** (Latin origin) means travelling through, by means of or by way of e.g. *They drove to London via Oxford. I will send that message via email. The boat was accessible via the ramp.*

Note: It is important to note the difference between abbreviations that are acceptable in formal writing or academic exercises and those used in social media and texting.

Bullet Points

A bullet point is a symbol, usually a dot, which is indented and placed before an important word, phrase or sentence in a list. Bullet points are used to emphasise and clarify key information making it easy to locate and read. You should use a colon at the end of an introduction to bullet points e.g. *The main points are:*

The main guidelines for using bullet points are:
- Use blank bullet points (dots) for things that are not in any particular sequence or order of importance. You could use alphabetical order to organise your list.
- Use numerals if the points are listed in order of importance.

- If a bullet point does not contain a complete sentence you do not need a capital letter to start or a full stop at the end.
- Bullet points should be roughly the same length.
- When using verbs to start bullet points, they should all be kept in the same tense.
- Be careful not to use too many bullet points or they may lose their impact and become boring.

Note: Bullet points should be kept consistent throughout. If you use a capital letter for the first word, a full stop at the end, a certain typeface or a verb to start then this should be repeated throughout the list.

Proofreading

Proofreading means checking written work for mistakes. Many of us make common errors such as omitting small words, writing in the wrong tense or using incorrect spellings. Proofreading can help to eliminate errors and set a high standard of writing which can convey efficiency, accuracy and reliability.

You should:
- Proofread your work to identify errors in spelling, punctuation, grammar, spacing, capital letters, words that have been omitted and sentences that don't make sense.
- Give your work to someone else to proofread. Another reader can often recognise illegible writing and identify parts that may be confusing or parts that they cannot understand.
- Check the overall sequence and structure of your writing.
- Always check homework or assignments for errors before handing them up for correction.

Spelling Strategies

People learn to spell words in many different ways e.g. *visually, orally or aurally*. It is important to appeal to as many of the senses as possible in order to improve success and cater for a variety of learning styles.

Some strategies to help you learn spellings:

- **Say each letter** when learning to spell a new word.
- **Say each word** when it is spelt.
- **Look, say, cover, write and check** is one recognised method of learning spellings. Examine the word, say the word, cover it and write it down. Then check if the spelling is correct. Repeat the process.
- **Write the word down**. The act of writing the word can help you to memorise the correct spelling.
- **Look at the word** you are writing. Examine it and ask yourself if it looks correct and if the shape of the word looks right.
- **Use colour** by writing sections of words or syllables in different colours. This can aid memory and help visual learners to spell more easily. The different colours highlight sections of the word and can make them easier to identify.
- **Use the words** by practicing them in short phrases, longer sentences and paragraphs. Repeated use of the words will help to aid memory.
- **Break large words into syllables (sounds)**. Write them down and look at them. This can make them easier to read and spell. e.g. *tem - per – a – ture*
- **Picture the word** in your head. Seeing the shape of the word in your 'mind's eye' can help when you are attempting to spell it.

- **Search for letter patterns and rhyming words.** Group rhyming words with similar spellings together. Remember, letters that go together in a pattern or rhyme can help us to learn spellings more easily.

  e.g. *adv_ice_   dev_ice_   d_ice_   sp_ice_*

- **Group words** with letters that look the same but sound different.

  e.g. *thr_ough_, en_ough_, c_ough_, alth_ough_*

- **Sound out** the words by pronouncing each syllable.

- **Identify the prefix and root word**

  e.g. *unhappy   root: happy + prefix: un = unhappy*

- **Identify the root word and suffix**

  e.g. *happiness   root: happy + suffix: ness = happiness*

- **Break up compound words.** Words such as newspaper, shoelace, pineapple or sometime are made up of two smaller words e.g. *pine + apple = pineapple.* Look for any compound words when you are learning to spell.

- **Pronounce silent letters.** When learning to spell words which contain silent letters it can help your memory if you pronounce all the silent letters. e.g. *Feb r_u_ ary, lam_b_, _k_nee*

- **Look for small words within larger words.** Examine words and look for smaller words within them. For example the word apparatus contains the smaller words 'par' 'rat', 'at', 'us'. Identifying smaller words within large words can help you to memorise letters and improve spelling.

- **Repeat** spelling exercises to reinforce memory.

- **Type words, sentences and paragraphs.** Use a keyboard to practice your spelling by typing the words.

- **Set your own targets** and learn one or two new words and then build on this. Don't expect to learn too many words at the one time. Imagine that you are learning a new language and consider how many new words you could learn to spell at one time.

- Compile a **personal dictionary** of words which you regularly need to use and spell. For example technical or subject vocabulary. Refer to this whenever you need to.
- **Learn some spelling rules**. e.g. *i before e except after c*
- **Underline** sections of a word where the spelling is confusing or difficult to remember.

Syllables

A syllable is one or more letters which make up a single unit of sound. The general rule for breaking words into separate syllables is that each syllable should contain at least one vowel or y. A syllable can be just one vowel or a group of letters.

- e.g. *tem – per – a – ture*   *nev – er – the – less*

Silent Letters

Silent letters are letters within a word which are not pronounced when you say the word.

Take note of any words which contain silent letters as this can help you to memorise the correct spelling. Pronouncing the silent letter can also help you to recall the correct spelling of the word.

Common Words with Silent Letters

autum**n**	**gh**ost	r**h**yme
bom**b**	hym**n**	r**h**ythm
bris**t**le	**k**nee	s**c**ience
ca**l**m	**k**nock	s**c**ene
ca**l**f	**k**not	si**g**n
chord	**k**nowledge	stoma**ch**

clim**b**	**k**now	su**b**tle
com**b**	**k**nuckle	wa**l**k
condem**n**	lim**b**	wa**t**ch
depo**t**	lis**t**en	**w**reck
desi**g**n	mus**c**le	**w**rench
dum**b**	mis**c**ellaneous	**w**rong
ex**h**ibition	**p**sychology	**w**rote
Feb**r**uary	**p**neumonia	**w**rist
forei**g**n	recei**p**t	**w**rite

Letter Patterns

Letter patterns are groups of letters that are repeated in different words. The words may or may not sound the same. Learning to recognise letter patterns can assist you with reading and spelling by helping you to recognise the look, the sound and the shape of the word.

Words with Letter Patterns

adv**ice**	dev**ice**	sp**ice**	ent**ice**
nour**ish**	styl**ish**	flour**ish**	tarn**ish**
accompl**ice**	prejud**ice**	liquor**ice**	just**ice**
transport	**trans**late	**trans**gress	**trans**lucent
m**illion**	b**illion**	tr**illion**	p**illion**
cons**ume**	ass**ume**	cost**ume**	res**ume**
c**ough**	th**ough**	en**ough**	thr**ough**
m**ove**	pr**ove**	gl**ove**	st**ove**
lo**tion**	mo**tion**	sta**tion**	rela**tion**

Compound Words

A compound word is made up of two or more smaller words which join together to make a new word. e.g. *sea + shell = seashell what + so + ever = whatsoever.* Noting how compound words are constructed can make it easier to learn how to spell them.

Examples of Compound Words

beeswax	eyebrow	pancake
blackberry	fingerprint	photocopy
candlestick	graveyard	pipeline
cookbook	greenhouse	sawdust
countersign	heirloom	seaweed
courthouse	lengthwise	superimpose
oatmeal	masterpiece	thumbtack
earache	milkshake	underestimate
earthquake	mudslide	weatherproof
evergreen	outnumber	woodwork

Words within Words

Small words are often hidden within larger words. Identifying these by underlining or highlighting them can help you to recognise, memorise and learn how to spell them.

Examples of Words within Larger Words

ap**parat**us	par	us
atmosp**here**	at	here
carbohyd**rate**	car	rate
mi**crow**ave	crow	wave
satu**rated**	sat	rated
temperature	temper	at
ve**get**ables	get	tables

Contractions

A contraction is a word or phrase that has been shortened by leaving a letter or letters out. In a contraction you must use an apostrophe in place of the missing letter or letters.

Common Contractions

are not / aren't	should have / should've
cannot / can't	should not / shouldn't
could not / couldn't	there is / there's
did not / didn't	they are / they're
do not / don't	they have / they've
does not / doesn't	was not / wasn't
have not / haven't	we are / we're
he is or he has / he's	we had or we would / we'd
he will / he'll	we have / we've
he would / he'd	we will / we'll
I am / I'm	were not / weren't
I had or I would / I'd	who are / who're
I have / I've	who have / who've
is not / isn't	will not / won't
it is or it has / it's	would have / would've
it will / it'll	would not / wouldn't
let us / let's	you are / you're
she had or she would / she'd	you had or you would / you'd
she is or she has/she's	you have / you've
she will / she'll	you will / you'll

Conjunctions

A conjunction is a word that joins two parts of a sentence together.

Common Conjunctions

also	nevertheless
although	nor
and	once
as	or
because	otherwise
but	since
consequently	so
despite	still
except	that
for	unless
furthermore	until
however	whereas
if	yet

Homophones

When two or more words have the same pronunciation but have different meanings they are called homophones. Some homophones have the same spelling. The context in which a homophone is used will help you to determine the correct meaning of the word.

Common Homophones

air / heir	key / quay	raise / rays
aisle / I'll	knead /need	read / reed
alter / altar	knew / new	right / write

ate / eight	know / no	rouse / rows
bail / bale	knows / nose	rung / wrung
band / banned	leak / leek	sale / sail
bare / bear	lessen / lesson	sea / see
beat / beet	licence / license	seam / seem
been / bean	loan / lone	side / sighed
boy / buoy	made / maid	soar / sore
bred / bread	mail / male	sole / soul
bye / buy	main / mane	some / sum
cheap / cheep	maize / maze	stair / stare
creak / creek	manner / manor	steak / stake
days / daze	mare / mayor	sweet / suite
dear / deer	meat / meet	tacks / tax
desert / dessert	medal / meddle	team / teem
dew / due	missed / mist	teas / tease
die / dye	muscle / mussel	there / they're/their
draft / draught	one / won	threw / through
fair / fare	pain / pane	thyme / time
feat / feet	peace / piece	to / too / two
find / fined	peak / peek	vain / vein
flair / flare	peal / peel	vale / veil
forth/fourth	plain / plane	waist / waste
foul / fowl	pole / poll	wait / weight
genes / jeans	principal / principle	way / weigh
hour / our	profit / prophet	we'd / weed
idle / idol	rain / reign	weak / week

Confusing Homophones

There, Their and They're

The homophones **there**, **their** and **they're** are often confused. Use:

- **there** when referring to a place or position
  e.g. *The books are kept on the shelf over there.*
- **their** to indicate ownership or possession
  e.g. *Their coats were left in the hall.*
- **they're** when used as a contraction for 'they are'
  e.g. *They're hoping to enter the competition tomorrow.*

Too, Two and To

The homophones **to, too and two** are often confused. Use:

- **too** when referring to also, as well as, or an excessive amount
  e.g. *The meal cost too much. I have those books too.*
- **two** when referring to the number 2
  e.g. *I have two black dogs.*
- **to** when using the word anywhere else
  e.g. *I went to the park. That belongs to Becky. You need to write to the doctor to make an appointment.*

Your, You're

The homophones **your** and **you're** are often confused. Use:

- **your** when you are using a pronoun
  e.g. *Bring your notes to the meeting tomorrow.*
  It is your turn to drive to work next week.
- **you're** (you are) when you are using a contraction
  e.g. *You're booked on the same flight as Michael.*
  'It's great that you're such a good little girl' said Ciara.

Difficult Words

I or Me?

I and **me** are both personal pronouns. Use:

- **I** when it is the subject of a sentence, in other words the person doing the action. e.g. *I am going to meet Shane at the station.*
- **me** when it is the object of the sentence, in other words the person the verb is acting upon. e.g. *He was talking to me earlier.*

Who, Which or That?

The words **who, which** and **that** often cause difficulty. Use:

- **who** or **whom** when referring to a person or people e.g. *It was Peter who broke the window.*
- **which** when referring to things e.g. *This is the hat which I bought.*
- **that** mainly for things but sometimes when referring to people. e.g. *These are the shoes that I want. This is the team that is going to win.*

Less or Fewer?

Use less when:

- you are referring to something that does not have a plural or can't be counted i.e. education, information, marketing, music, evidence, honesty, news etc.

  e.g. *Children were less educated in the past.*

  If they gave us less information this would be easier to do.

Use fewer when:

- you are referring to plural people or things i.e. *boys, hats, books, cats etc.*

  e.g. *There are fewer people going on holidays these days.*

  Children got far fewer presents in the past.

A or An?

Whether to use **'a'** or **'an'** before a word depends on the pronunciation of the first syllable of the word. It does not depend on how the word is spelt. The general rule is:

Use 'a' before a word when:

- the word starts with a **consonant** sound
  e.g. *a dog, a brown fox, a rainy day, a hospital etc.*
- it begins with the letters 'eu' pronounced with the long 'u' sound
  e.g. *a European, a eulogy, a euphemism, a eucalyptus tree*
- the letter 'u' at the beginning of the word sounds like 'eu'
  e.g. *a union, a unit, a uniform, a university, a unique feature*

Use 'an' before a word when:

- the word starts with a **vowel** sound
  e.g. *an apple, an exercise, an onion, an urban setting etc.*
- the word starts with a silent 'h'
  e.g. *an heir, an honour, an hour, an honest person*

Among or Between?

The general rule is to:

Use between when:

- referring to two items, two people or two groups
  e.g. *The only difference between you and me is our height.*
  I will divide the chocolate between the boys and the girls.
  He sat between his colleagues. (implies two colleagues)

Use among when:

- referring to groups of more than two
  e.g. *The only difference among us is our height.*
  We will divide the chocolate among the group.
  He sat among his colleagues. (implies more than two colleagues)

Confusing Words

Some words sound alike but have very different meanings. This can often lead to confusion when trying to select the right spelling and most appropriate word to use in the correct context.

Some Confusing Words

accept	except
is a verb. It means to receive something or take delivery of something. e.g. *He agreed to accept the parcel when the postman called.*	means apart from or excluding. e.g. *We are all going to work except for Peter who is sick today.*
adverse	**averse**
means preventing, unpleasant or unfavourable. e.g. *We could not travel today due to the adverse weather.*	means dislike, unwilling, hesitant or loath. It is normally followed by the preposition 'to' e.g. *The manager was averse to sharing a joke. He was averse to fun.*
advise	**advice**
is a verb which means to give council or tell someone what their best course of action might be. e.g. *I would advise that student to apply for the college course as soon as possible.*	is a noun which means suggestion, recommendation, opinion or view offered on something. e.g. *I took his advice when he told me to go to the meeting.*
affect	**effect**
is a verb which means to make a difference or influence. e.g. *The bright lights had begun to affect my eyes.*	means result of, as a consequence, or outcome. e.g. *If you switch the lights out you will see the full effect of the fire.*

affluent	effluent
means rich, prosperous or wealthy. e.g. *Many families were affluent before the recession.*	means waste, sewage or liquid pollution. e.g. *The effluent seeped from the factory into the river before anyone noticed.*
allude	**elude**
means suggest or hint or refer to indirectly. e.g. *The manager briefly alluded to the fact that I had missed the meeting.*	means to escape, avoid, evade or dodge. e.g. *He ran as fast as he could but the top prize always eluded him.*
all together	**altogether**
means everyone or everything together as one. e.g. *When we were all together we had a great time.*	means totally, entirely or completely. e.g. *He drove in with a different model of car altogether.*
alternate	**alternative**
means going back and forward between two things. e.g. *He was advised to alternate between standing and sitting.*	means another choice. e.g. *The bus took an alternative route when the road was blocked.*
aloud	**allowed**
means out loud or audibly or can be heard. e.g. *As he read the words aloud his audience laughed heartily.*	means authorised or permitted. e.g. *The teenagers were allowed to eat their lunch early.*
altar	**alter**
means a religious table usually seen in a church. e.g. *The altar had lovely candles and flowers on it. The bride walked to the altar.*	means to change or amend something. e.g. *I asked the dressmaker to alter my trousers as I had lost weight.*

apart means in pieces. e.g. *The toy fell apart when Anne dropped it on the tiled floor.*	**a part** means a section or piece of something. e.g. *I got a part in the play.*
bazaar means a market place. e.g. *There were lots of people shopping in the bazaar.*	**bizarre** means unusual, strange or odd. e.g. *The old woman was wearing a bizarre hat with purple ribbons and a blue veil.*
company's is a possessive word. e.g. *The company's computers have all been updated.*	**companies** is the plural word for company. e.g. *The companies on the industrial estate are kept busy.*
compliment means praise or flatter. e.g. *I thought I would compliment him on his great speech.* *He complimented me on my piano recital.*	**complement** means quantity or something that goes well with something else. e.g. *The full complement of staff was in today.* *The red tie was the perfect complement to his navy suit.*
council means a group of elected people, assembly or committee. e.g. *The council voted to increase the parking charge.*	**counsel** means advice, consultation, suggested opinion or guarding your thoughts. e.g. *The woman was entitled to legal counsel.*
current means happening now or flow of air or water e.g. *The current recession is a disaster.* *The current was too strong for the swimmer.*	**currant** means a dried grape. e.g. *As I was putting dried fruit in the cake the currant fell on the floor.*

defuse means to remove a fuse or make something less dangerous. e.g. *The army was called in to defuse the landmine.*	**diffuse** as a verb means to spread out. e.g. *You can use the burner to diffuse essential oils in the room.*
elicit means to provoke, cause or produce a certain reaction. e.g. *The journalist asked probing questions in order to elicit a negative response.*	**illicit** means unlawful or illegal. e.g. *The illicit fuel was smuggled across the border.*
everyday is an adjective and means commonplace or ordinary occurrence. e.g. *These are my everyday clothes.*	**every day** means each individual day. e.g. *I take my dog for a walk every day.*
everyone means all the people together. e.g. *I will email everyone when I get the results.*	**every one** means each one individually. e.g. *I counted every one of the folders before I left them into the office.*
desert means to leave or abandon someone or something / a hot dry empty place. e.g. *Camels live in the desert. He deserted his wife last year.*	**dessert** is a sweet dish eaten after a meal. e.g. *I chose toffee pudding for my dessert.*
imply means to suggest something indirectly. e.g. *Her tone of voice seemed to imply that she was very happy with the news.*	**infer** means to draw a conclusion. e.g. *I could infer the meaning of what he was saying when he concluded the speech.*

licence	license
is a noun which means an official permit to do something. e.g. *He got a licence to fish in the local river.*	is a verb which means to give permission. e.g. *I went to the council office to license my car. The officer licenses dogs here.*
maybe means perhaps. e.g. *Maybe we'll go the cinema on Friday.*	**may be** means possibly and is similar to might be or could be. e.g. *The doctor may be away next week.*
practice is a noun. e.g. *The yellow book sets out best practice for health and safety in the computer room.*	**practise** is a verb which means to perform something. e.g. *I practise the guitar. You are practising the piano.*
principal means the most important or main thing / the most senior person. e.g. *The principal said I could have a day off school for the wedding.*	**principle** means a standard, code or belief. e.g. *The core principles of the organisation include equality, trust and respect.*
sometime means any time at all. e.g. *We must meet up sometime soon.*	**some time** means a specific amount of time. e.g. *It will take some time to fix that puncture.*
whose is the possessive form of who. e.g. *Whose bag is blocking the corridor?*	**who's** is a contraction. It means who is or who has. e.g. *Do you know who's on duty today?*

Oral, Aural and Visual Communication Skills

The broad view of literacy includes oral, aural and visual skills. Practicing these forms of communication can encourage oral fluency, creative thinking and promote the use of new vocabulary. Observing body language and gesture can heighten our awareness of how we can physically demonstrate and express our own feelings, moods, attitudes and emotions.

Developing observation and visual skills can improve memory and help us to identify the finer points of visual images. Developing active listening can help us to improve learning and expand recognition of sound and rhythm used in reading, poetry and spellings.

Tone of Voice

Tone of voice can convey a variety of different messages such as anger, humour, sarcasm or sincerity. A person's accent and the volume of his/her voice can also give the listener clues about the speaker and the message he/she is conveying. The way you say something can change the meaning of words so it is important to match your tone with the message you are trying to convey.

- e.g. *'I would love to go to the zoo'* said in a sarcastic voice may give the impression that you would not like to go to the zoo. The same sentence expressed in an excited tone could mean the opposite and that you would love to go to the zoo.

It is important to use the correct volume with your voice. Too loud a voice can give the impression that you are angry or aggressive and too quiet may indicate that you are being secretive. Using volume inappropriately can make people uncomfortable. e.g. *speaking loudly in a quiet place such as a library or church.*

Consider tone and volume for the following voices:

- angry voice
- voice used when talking to a small child
- sleepy voice
- sarcastic voice
- sincere voice
- in a rush voice
- voice when terrified of something
- totally bored voice
- very excited voice

Think about the impression you give when you use each of these tones of voice.

Conversation Skills

Conversation is a social skill and an art that can be mastered by learning some techniques and practising them. Clear and correct speech can help to create a good impression of ourselves. It can help with avoiding misunderstandings, expressing opinions and making new friends.

When people meet for the first time and engage in conversation they should:

- Introduce themselves by saying their name, smiling, asking questions and showing an interest in the other person.
- Shake hands firmly if appropriate.
- Maintain conversation by listening intently and using empathic body language like nodding, saying mmm ... etc.
- Ask open questions, use friendly small talk and use ice breakers such as the weather, the occasion or event etc.
- Treat each other the way they would like to be treated.
- Repeat the person's name occasionally.

- Listen to each other and stay interested.
- Draw attention to anything that they both have in common.
- End the conversation with something friendly e.g. *'nice talking to you', 'nice to meet you', 'thanks' etc.* and perhaps arrange another meeting.

When people engage in conversation they should not:
- Dominate or intimidate each other.
- Use rude or foul language.
- Interrupt, talk over or criticise others.
- Engage in discussion on strongly held political opinion, religion, or any controversial or sensitive subject.

Public Speaking

Speaking in front of a small or large group can be daunting but practice diminishes nerves and can greatly boost self-confidence and self-esteem. A talk is informal while a speech is a more formal delivery of a message. They both need an introduction, main body and a conclusion.

Preparing a speech or a talk:
- Select the topic you wish to speak about.
- Find out how much time you have to speak. Remember that a short talk can have more impact than a long ramble.
- Take time to research your topic.
- Write down the main points and keep it simple.
- Identify your target audience and consider cultural sensitivity e.g. *ethnicity, beliefs or customs.*
- Tailor your speech to the needs of your audience e.g. *If you are speaking to children do not use complicated words.*

- Structure the content of the talk in a logical sequence which is easy to follow. Have a clear beginning, middle and end.
- Use small prompt cards if you wish. Prompt cards are small cards where you can write a summary of the main points of your presentation. You shouldn't read directly from them, but rather refer to them every so often to help you keep on track. Different colour cards can help to keep you speaking in the correct sequence.
- Stand up straight and make eye contact with the audience in a confident manner.
- Practise, rehearse and time yourself.
- Practise in front of someone and ask for feedback.
- Ensure that visual aids are relevant and support what you are saying e.g. *photographs, PowerPoint etc.*
- If using visual aids remember to check that the venue has the appropriate equipment e.g. *computer, sound, screen etc.*
- Be aware of the signals your posture and body language give.
- Ensure that you project your voice so that you can be heard at the back of the room.
- Remember to pronounce words correctly. If in doubt check them out beforehand.
- Use a varied tone of voice and be careful not to repeat words or sounds such as 'umm', 'right', 'now', 'ok' etc.
- Pace your talk at an appropriate speed so that the audience can follow the sequence and understand what you are saying.
- Incorporate humour where appropriate.

Note: Be careful not to overuse visual aids such as photographs and Microsoft PowerPoint slides as they may distract or confuse your audience and become a barrier to the delivery of your key message.

Visual Aids and Presentations

There are many different types of visual aids such as flip charts, photographs, digital slides, DVDs etc. When using visual aids with a speech or presentation you must ensure that they are relevant and support what you are saying.

Visual communication aids such as Microsoft PowerPoint enable you to produce multimedia presentations using slides. These visual aids are tools which should only be used to reinforce your presentation.

Guidelines for preparing a PowerPoint presentation:

- Identify the key point/s that you wish to present.
- Identify your target audience and consider their concentration span and level of knowledge about your subject.
- Keep slides simple using large images, large text and a small number of fonts. The font is the style and size of the lettering.
- Headings should be approximately 36 - 40pt.
- The main body size should be at least 24pt.
- Limit bullet points to approximately 3 – 6 per slide.
- Use lower case letters unless a capital letter is specifically required. (see p.9)
- Choose a colour scheme that sets the text in high contrast to the background colour in order to ensure readability.
- Consider using charts, uncomplicated graphics and images.
- Remember that images can evoke more powerful emotions than text and this can help to engage your audience.
- Use single words or phrases rather than sentences.
- Leave space on your slides as overcrowding can make them less interesting and confuse your message.
- Do not overuse special effects such as animation or sound as these may become distracting.
- Avoid standard templates and think creatively.

- Arrange slides in a logical sequence.
- Conclude with a summary, question/s or thoughts and ensure that your last slide leaves an impact on your audience.
- Always proofread your presentation to check for any errors.

Guidelines for presentations:
- Know your subject well.
- Dress appropriately and be aware of the impression that your appearance creates.
- Use positive body language to demonstrate control. e.g. *eye contact, facial expression, body posture, etc.* (see p.71)
- Practice, rehearse and time yourself to ensure a smooth professional delivery.
- Check that the venue you are presenting in has the appropriate equipment for your needs e.g. *computer, microphone, screen etc.*
- Do not stand in front of the screen - be aware of the position your audience is sitting in and don't block their line of vision.
- If you intend to take questions from the audience let them know at the beginning when this will happen e.g. *at the end of your presentation.*
- Use your slides to support your narration rather than reading directly from them.
- Keep your tone of voice relaxed but professional.
- Speak slowly and clearly and be sure that your voice can be heard at the back of the room or hall.
- Avoid using slang, clichés or inappropriate language.
- Be sensitive to local/global culture, practices and beliefs.

Telephone or Audio Conferencing

When engaging in non-visual communication your tone of voice is critical as the other person cannot see who is speaking. They can only get an impression of you from your voice. It is often the way you say something rather than what you say that leaves an impression.

Important points to remember:

- Prepare what you are going to say before connecting to the person.
- Select an appropriate greeting to start the conversation.
- Sit up straight so as not to constrict your voice.
- Speak clearly and distinctly.
- Do not speak too quickly.
- Maintain a polite tone of voice keeping it warm and friendly.
- Do not use any slang, clichés or bad language.
- Listen to the other person attentively and do not interrupt.
- Have a pen and paper ready before making or taking a call so that you can record information such as names, numbers and what has been said or agreed.
- Take a note of the name of the person/s, the date and the time of the call.
- Do not make interfering noise e.g. *shuffle paper, click your pen, carry on side conversations, eat or drink while talking etc.*
- With remote/global communication check the time zone of the country where the person is located.

Note: When contacting someone for the first time it is essential to make a good impression. Remember that you only get one chance to make a first impression.

Role Play

Role play means acting out a situation. You must change your normal behaviour to imitate a character different to your own.

Role play facilitates the development of speaking, dialogue, voice projection and confidence and can involve conflict, persuasion, problem solving and discussion. A role play can be recorded and then critiqued and discussed.

For a role play you need to:
- Select a **topic.** e.g. *An Accident in the Workroom*
- Choose the **setting.** i.e. *where the scene takes place*
- Plan the number of **roles** needed. e.g. *the manager, the injured person, the medical team etc.*
- **Allocate** the roles to participants.
- **Plan** what happens to each character.

To organise a role play:
- Elect someone to organise the role play.
- Choose a (preferably real life) scenario and describe it to your partner or team.
- Brainstorm about the vocabulary needed for the scenario that you have chosen.
- Decide on a time frame for the role play.
- Use some props to make it more interesting. Props such as reading glasses, overcoats, hats etc. can help to set the scene and make it more fun.
- Participants can be divided into pairs or small groups to act out the role play. Alternatively, one group can act out the scenario while others can listen and observe.
- A discussion around problem solving could follow the role play.

The following points will help you to plan your role play:
- What age is the character you are playing?
- What is your character wearing?
- What tone of voice would your character use?
- What is your relationship with the other characters in the role play?
- What time of the day or year is the role play set in?
- What story are you trying to convey?
- Are there any props you can use to set the scene?

Possible role play situations:
- Someone has cut themselves in the workroom while using a machine. What do you do and say?
- Your new mobile phone is faulty. Return to where you bought it and make a complaint.
- You are involved in a team project. Your team wants to do a project on wind farms but you want to do the project on the rainforest. Persuade them to agree with your idea.

Debate

A debate is a competition between two teams with opposing views on a subject. Debating can develop the skills of reasoned argument, persuasion and problem solving. Good oral presentation can foster leadership and improve interpersonal skills.

To organise a debate:
- Select **two teams** each comprising of two or three people.
- A **topic** should be given to the teams in advance, in order that they may research the subject and prepare their argument and obtain facts to back up their views.

- **Ground rules** should be established e.g. *stay with the subject, do not get drawn into personal attacks, do not use abusive comments or foul language etc.*
- The **time allowed** for each team member to speak should be decided beforehand.
- Remind teams to use **persuasive body language** while presenting their points e.g. *using their hands or gesturing.*
- Remind participants that **voice projection** and clarity of speech are important in order for them to be heard and understood.
- Ask teams to include some **appropriate humour** if possible.
- One team should speak for the motion and the other against the motion.
- When the debate is about to start the team members should be **introduced** to the audience and their position on the argument announced.
- A **timekeeper** should be chosen to ensure accurate timing and this person can stop anyone who runs overtime.
- Each speaker on both teams is generally given an **equal amount of time** to talk.
- The debate should start with a member of the **supporting team speaking first** and a member of the opposing team speaking next. Alternate between the teams until everyone has finished.
- A speech should **never be interrupted**.
- **Questions** from the judges or the audience can be asked at the end of a round.
- The audience can judge by **voting** to decide on the winning team **or** a panel of judges can be selected to do this **or** alternatively the facilitator can decide which team had the most persuasive arguments.

Non-Verbal Skills

Listening Skills

The skill of effective listening is often overlooked in favour of other forms of communication and yet it is one of the most important elements of gathering information and learning.

Listening is the skill of receiving a message accurately. Hearing and listening are two different things. We can hear sounds such as someone talking without actually listening to them. Listening needs concentration and this is called active listening.

To improve your listening skills:

- Identify barriers to listening. e.g. *background noise, mobile phones, view from a window, others moving about etc.*
- Actively ignore distractions or remove them where possible.
- Stop talking.
- Focus on the speaker.
- Engage in active listening by paying attention and concentrating on the message the other person is trying to convey.
- When someone is talking do not interrupt or talk over them.
- Wait until the other person has finished speaking before you clarify any points with them.
- Avoid selective hearing where you only listen to and interpret parts of a message that you feel are relevant to you.
- Empathise with what the person is saying by nodding, gesturing or making encouraging noises like 'mmm' or 'I see'.
- Listen with your eyes as well as your ears in order to pick up subtle messages and non-verbal clues e.g. *body language*

Visual Skills

Our world is full of visual images ranging from photographs, computer graphics, films, television, advertising, artwork and much more. The way we interpret image and interact with our visual environment is an important part of who we are.

Visual awareness includes the interpretation of signs and symbols such as safety signage, road signage, logos etc. These offer an alternative way of conveying a message rather than using words. Signs and symbols are a universal language which can convey messages to all people of all nationalities.

Visual memory is the ability to conjure up images of prior learning and prior experiences e.g. *images in books, stories, films and images of events and experiences.*

Improve visual memory by using:

- **memory games** – e.g. *select some objects, examine them, then remove and write down as many as you can remember.*
- **spot the difference** puzzles e.g. *comparing two pictures and identifying any differences.*
- **photographs** – Examine photographs and interpret images. Ask yourself questions such as: Who is in the picture? Where is it located? What is happening? What are the people saying? Is it a good photograph? What is your opinion?
- **eyewitness** statements – e.g. *accident report.*
- **maze puzzles** – Find your way through the maze.
- **images** – Look at a picture for a set amount of time and then answer some questions about it. Record details.
- **paintings** – Interpret a painting by decoding symbols and using inference and deduction to deepen understanding.
- **cartoons** – Ask yourself what is happening? Why is it funny?

- **posters** – Examine and interpret images in posters. Ask questions such as – What message does it convey? Is there a slogan? Is there a logo? What colours are used and why?
- **advertisements** – Examine and decode subtle messages. Ask yourself questions such as - What are they selling? What is in the background? Who are they targeting? Is there a slogan? What colours are used and why? Is there a brand name? Who would it appeal to? What imagery does it contain? Does it depict a certain lifestyle? How does it make you feel?

Dress Code

People form opinions and make judgements about us based on our appearance. Your clothing can convey non-verbal clues about your character, emotions and status in life. It is important to match an occasion such as an interview or wedding with the appropriate attire.

When choosing how to dress remember that:

- The type of clothing you wear conveys a message to others and may hold the only clues to your character.
- Accessories such as jewellery, hats, bags or shoes should always be appropriate for the occasion and chosen carefully.
- Dressing down can express or indicate an attitude of laziness and inefficiency while overdressing could convey attention seeking or aloofness.
- Dressing appropriately for an occasion can convey intelligence, efficiency, style and professionalism.
- If you are wearing a uniform, you are sending out a message about your organisation, their ethos and their brand. Many organisations use uniforms to make them easily identifiable and also to convey a sense of equality, team spirit, pride and commonality.

Body Language

Body language is an important part of communication. Being able to interpret gestures, posture and physical signs of a person's emotions or mood can build confidence and self-awareness. Even a subtle movement such as a slightly raised eyebrow can convey a message. Remember that body language and posture can be interpreted in various ways in different cultures.

Body language skills exercises:

- Use facial expression to convey non-verbal messages e.g. *frowning, smiling etc.* to underpin what you are saying.
- Reinforce what you are saying by using gestures e.g. *pointing a finger, waving, shrugging, nodding etc.* to strengthen your message.
- Use posture e.g. *the way you stand, sit or move your body etc.* to strengthen the impact of your message.
- Watch a TV programme or political interview with the sound turned off. Examine the body language and decide what is happening and what the people might be saying.
- Identify a range of non-verbal signals from photographs and discuss what they mean. Discuss the connection between body language and verbal communication.
- Select images of facial expression and posture from newspapers or magazines and try to identify them.
- Examine images of facial expressions and body language on the Internet and discuss them.
- Make some facial expressions e.g. *anger, happiness, surprise etc.* Ask others to guess what expression is being portrayed.
- Mime (act without words) a situation with a partner. Ask others to write down what they think is happening and then see if they interpreted your body language correctly.

Personal Space

Personal space is an invisible boundary. The immediate area surrounding a person is known as their personal space. This is the distance between two people where one person feels comfortable talking to another. If this area is encroached upon, it can make the person feel uncomfortable or anxious.

Personal space exercises:

- Arrange participants in pairs. Get one person to approach another face to face. Ask them to decide at which point they feel that their personal space is being invaded.
- Ask one person to approach another from the side and see if this is different from a face-to-face approach.
- Carry out the same exercises asking the stationary person to close their eyes and sense the approach of the other person.

Eye Contact

The conventions on eye contact vary across cultures but in the western world, eye contact can convey sincerity, friendship, trust and respect. Avoiding eye contact can give the wrong impression such as being untruthful, hiding something, disinterest or shyness.

Eyes and eyebrows can express energy and emotion and these can be used to reinforce a point. Be careful not to hold direct eye contact for too long as this may seem like staring. Look away occasionally.

To improve skills of communicating with eye contact:

- Pass a message on to someone who is not looking at you. For example they could be looking at the ground instead. Consider how this makes you feel.
- Keep looking at someone directly. Ask them how long it takes for the stare to become uncomfortable.
- Pass a message on to someone while making eye contact and smiling. Ask the person how that makes them feel.

Digital Communications

Digital Literacy

There are two ways that we can represent ourselves in terms of literacy within digital media: 'casual literacy' and 'formal literacy'.

Casual literacy refers to informal and sometimes sloppy writing which can often include abbreviations, clichés or even slang. It does not conform to the general rules of writing where correct use of punctuation and grammar is adhered to.

Casual literacy is acceptable:
- when communicating with friends
- when communicating with family
- on social networking sites
- when texting

Formal literacy requires correct grammar, spelling and punctuation and should portray an accurate and professional image.

Formal literacy should be used for:
- all written school work including projects and homework
- all college exercises
- all work related documents, emails, letters, applications etc.

Using poor grammar and spelling in emails, letters and other formal situations can convey carelessness and unreliability and portray a lack of efficiency and accuracy. For example, advertising an item with information that is misspelt can give prospective buyers the impression that the item is faulty or of poor quality.

Composing Formal Emails

The key to successful emailing is choosing the appropriate form and tone of writing for the particular recipient of your message.

When emailing a colleague or business contact, the message must conform to the correct rules of punctuation, grammar and spelling. A formal email must be concise and clearly laid out. It is similar to a letter but it should be short, so if a lot of information needs to be included this should be added as an attachment.

Guidelines for sending formal emails:

- Take note of who the recipient of your message is and what type of relationship you have with them.
- If you are emailing someone for the first time you should follow the guidelines for a formal letter and explain at the start of your message who you are and why you are contacting them.
- Check that you have typed the correct email address.
- Use a short and accurate subject heading which is clearly related to the topic/s in the email.
- You should use a greeting to begin your message.
- The greeting in your message should always match the relationship that you have with the recipient. In a business context try to use the person's title and name e.g. *Dear Mr Jones.* For more than one recipient address all of them together e.g. *Dear colleagues.*
- State the purpose of your email in the first line.
- Try to be specific, get to the point quickly and don't ramble.
- Do not use all block capital letters in a message. Use capitals only where they are needed e.g. *the start of a sentence, names etc.* Otherwise use all lower case letters.

- Avoid using abbreviated text, bad language, slang, jargon or clichés.
- Ensure that the language used in the email is respectful.
- Be careful that your message does not sound too abrupt. Remember, an email does not contain other communication clues such as body language or tone of voice so it could be misinterpreted.
- Read your message before sending it and try to gauge the tone of it. You can't take an email back once it is sent.
- Take care to proofread your message to eliminate poor grammar, missing words or misspellings as these can convey carelessness, lack of professionalism and lack of respect for the recipient. Take your time and spellcheck your message.
- Be polite. Use please and thank you just as you would if you were speaking directly to the person.
- Sign a formal email in the same manner as you would with a formal letter. e.g. *Yours sincerely, Yours faithfully etc.*
- For a more informal ending you could use Regards, Kind regards or Best wishes etc.

Note: It is difficult to convey tone, emotion, sarcasm, humour or sincerity in an email. The recipient may misinterpret what you are trying to say in a message. For messages that require many nuances it may be more appropriate to talk over the phone or meet and speak in person.

Internet Safety

The growth of Internet usage worldwide brings risks to our safety such as identity theft, cyberbullying and unauthorised access to personal information. Most schools and businesses have their own guidelines and social media policy on Internet usage. It is important to familiarise yourself with these in order to maximise personal safety and minimise security risks.

Remember:

- You should treat contacts on the Internet as complete strangers unless you have met them in person. Do not give any personal information, passwords or photographs belonging to you or your friends or family to anyone you meet on the Internet.
- Not all Internet sites contain reliable information.
- The Internet provides instant communication so it is important that all writing should be proofread before uploading or sending it.
- Nothing is private on the Internet. Once someone posts a message or sends an email it cannot be taken back or deleted.
- Information and images on the Internet generally belong to the person who created them. While some sites provide free information and images it is important to check the copyright terms and conditions before using them.
- When using information directly from a website it should be cited so the author is credited with the work.
- When making comments on social media sites, it is important that they are not misinterpreted as something else e.g. *racist or sexist comments.*
- Do not download or install software if you are unsure of its credibility.
- Safety, privacy and ethics are all important when using the Internet as you could be at risk of illegal activity or abuse.

Examination Vocabulary

Exam Word	Meaning
analyse	investigate and explore in detail in order to explain and interpret
appraise	estimate or judge the quality
approximate	almost exact, estimated or very similar
assess	consider, judge or weigh up the importance or worth of something
bisect	divide into two parts
briefly	short or a few words
characteristics	features or qualities
comment	give your opinion or reaction
compare	show similarities and differences
compulsory	must do or is required
construct	build or make according to specific requirements or instructions
contrast	point out the differences
create	make, build or produce
deduct (maths)	take away or subtract
define	give the exact meaning of
describe	write a detailed account or explanation or say what something looks like
design	make a creative plan or creative picture or drawing
diagram	a drawing, plan, map or chart or a drawing with labels explaining what everything is
differentiate	explain the difference
disadvantage	drawback or weakness
discuss	talk about arguments for and against and consider all possibilities - support these with

	examples or evidence
dissect	systematically cut up into pieces in order to examine or study
distinguish	show the difference or tell apart
draw (art)	make or create a drawing
draw (conclusions)	read to understand and then make a judgement based on this
elevation	front view
estimate	roughly judge the size, number, quantity or extent of something
evidence	proof or verification
examine	look at carefully or inspect
explain	give an explanation or make clear
extract	remove or take out
extract (writing)	passage, piece of writing or quotation
highlight	mark certain parts or draw attention to
identify	name or pick out the key things
illustrate	explain and make clear by giving examples
Illustrate (art)	make a drawing of
indicate	show or point out
interpret	explain the meaning in your own words
investigate	examine systematically or make a detailed inquiry
justify	provide evidence supporting an argument, point of view or idea.
list	make a list of items, words or comments arranged one after the other
locate	search and find
method	way of doing something
name	give the title of

narrate	tell or give an account of
outline	give a general summary or give the main features without the minor detail
outline (drawing)	draw around or sketch out
passage (writing)	piece of writing or text
precaution	safety measure
proportion	a part considered in relation to the whole
propose	offer or put forward an idea
prove	show that something is true by providing evidence
recall	remember or recollect
relate (story or event)	tell or describe
relate (between things)	establish or show the connection between two or more things
reproduce	produce again or do again
review	check or go over something again
recommend	suggest what you think is best
sketch (art)	rough drawing
solve	work out the correct answer to a problem
source	start or cause of or beginning
state	express clearly by giving short clear answers
suggest	put forward an idea or propose something
suitable	appropriate or fitting
summarise	give the main points or ideas without the smaller details
topic	subject or theme
trace	follow the history, development or progress of
visualise	form a mental picture, imagine or visualise

British and American English - Spelling Differences

British and American English spelling can be different. Some of the most common differences are listed below:

words ending in **re** and **er**:

British English	American English
cent**re**	cent**er**
fib**re**	fib**er**
lit**re**	lit**er**
manoeuv**re**	maneuv**er**
theat**re**	theat**er**

words ending in **our** and **or**:

British English	American English
col**our**	col**or**
flav**our**	flav**or**
hum**our**	hum**or**
lab**our**	lab**or**
neighb**our**	neighb**or**
od**our**	od**or**
rum**our**	rum**or**

words ending in **iour** and **ior**:

British English	American English
behav**iour**	behav**ior**
sav**iour**	sav**ior**

words ending in **ise** and **ize**:

British English	American English
author**ise**	author**ize**
fertil**ise**	fertil**ize**
organ**ise**	organ**ize**
recogn**ise**	recogn**ize**
vandal**ise**	vandal**ize**

words ending in **yse** and **yze**:

British English	American English
anal**yse**	anal**yze**
paral**yse**	paral**yze**

words ending in **ce** and **se**:

British English	American English
defen**ce**	defen**se**
offen**ce**	offen**se**

words ending in **ogue** and **og**:

British English	American English
dial**ogue**	dial**og**
epil**ogue**	epil**og**
monol**ogue**	monol**og**

Some other common words with spelling differences:

British English	American English
aesthetic	**es**thetic
age**i**ng	ag**i**ng
alumi**nium**	alumi**num**
dia**ll**ed	dia**l**ed
f**oet**al	f**et**al
gr**ey**	gr**ay**
jew**ell**ery	jew**el**ery
ma**noeu**vre	ma**neu**ver
medi**ae**val	medi**e**val
m**ou**ld	m**o**ld
pl**ough**	pl**ow**
sul**ph**ur	sul**f**ur
syphon	**sip**hon
trav**ell**ing	trav**el**ing
tyre	**ti**re
yo**gh**urt	yo**g**urt